Change Your Perspective Change Your Life

Discover How To Reduce Your Suffering And Enjoy Your Life By Mastering Your Emotions

Sensei Paul David

Copyright Page

Change Your Perspective Change Your Life: Discover How To Reduce Your Suffering And Enjoy Your Life By Mastering Your Emotions, by Sensei Paul David

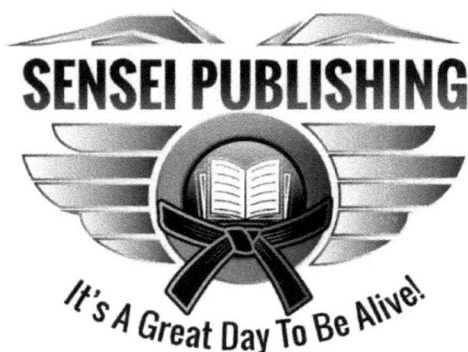

SENSEI PUBLISHING

It's A Great Day To Be Alive!

www.senseipublishing.com

@senseipublishing
#senseipublishing

Get/Share Our FREE All-Ages Mental Health Book Now!

FREE Self-Development Book for Every Family

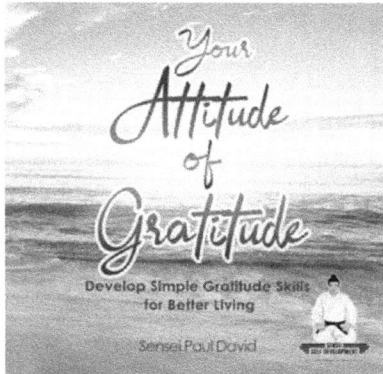

Click Below or Search Amazon for Another Book In This Series

Join Our Publishing Journey!

If you would like to receive FUTURE FREE BOOKS and get to know us better, please click www.senseipublishing.com and join our newsletter by entering your email address in the pop-up box.

Follow Our Blog: senseipauldavid.ca

Follow/Like/Subscribe: Facebook, Instagram, YouTube: @senseipublishing

Scan the QR Code with your phone or tablet

to follow us on social media: Like / Subscribe / Follow

Thank You from The Author: Sensei Paul David

Before we dive in, I would like to thank you for picking up this book from among the many other similar books out there. Thank you for choosing to invest in my book. That means everything to me.

Now that you are here, I ask you to stick with me as we take your self-discovery journey together. I promise to make our time together valuable and worthwhile.

In the pages ahead, you will find some areas of information and practices more helpful than others - and that is great! I encourage you to apply what works best for you. You will benefit from the knowledge that you gain and the ensuing exciting transformation of character.

Enjoy!

Table of Contents

Chapter Seven: Maximizing Happiness 56

Chapter Eight: Don't Be The Aggressor! 65

Conclusion 74

References 76

Foreword

Life is mystical to people who do not understand its principles and how to navigate them. However, it is full of bliss for those who know how to turn their lemons into lemonades. The truth about life is that pain is inevitable. There will always be circumstances that will hurt us and make us wish we never made certain decisions. Nonetheless, you can always find happiness amid this turbulence when you gain mastery over your thoughts.

In *Change Your Perspective; Change Your Life,* Sensei Paul practically explains the hidden truth that our emotions are not as real as we think. Most times, it is not your experiences that are frustrating you but your perception of the circumstances you find yourself in. Sometimes, a divorce might be a blessing in disguise. For example, some people have lived happier and more meaningful life after they left an abusive spouse.

Every negative event will hurt you but many such occurrences will be the dawn of a new era in your life when you have the right perspective. This book is packed with valuable lessons and tips that will improve your emotional intelligence and help you gain mastery over the art of recovering from setbacks.

Introduction

"Watch your thoughts, they become words; watch your words, they become actions; watch your actions, they become habits; watch your habits, they become character; watch your character, for it becomes your destiny."

Frank Outlaw

One of the most important lessons I learned early in life was that my emotions are products of my perspective. Don't get me wrong; I do not mean to say that there is no such thing as a sad event. Of course, certain situations are unprecedentedly disappointing, such as the loss of a loved one, a divorce, the loss of one's job, etc.

No one desires such situations and, naturally, we are disappointed when they occur. Nonetheless, despite how hurt we are by those experiences, what determines whether they will make us suffer depends on our perception of the situation. If you perceive an event as an occurrence that will ruin your life, you will struggle to recover from it.

On the other hand, when you convince yourself that an occurrence is a blessing in disguise that will help you to live your best life, you will find yourself enjoying a new lease on life. If you desire to suffer less, despite experiencing painful events, this is the right book for you; I guarantee that you will thoroughly enjoy this journey. I am so excited to get started! Today is a good day!

Chapter One: Pain Is Inevitable

"Pain is inevitable. Suffering is optional."
Dalai Lama

We live in an imperfect world. Therefore, it is unrealistic to expect to live without pain and challenges. When people make marriage vows, they declare their commitment to stay with one another during turbulence and affluence. Sadly, that is not always the reality because many people jump ship the moment a storm is looming. We might not like it but pain and adversity are part and parcel of life. This reality is the focal point of this chapter.

No Anesthesia

William T.G. Morton, a Boston dentist, used sulfuric ether on October 16, 1846, to anesthetize a man during the removal of a vascular tumor from his neck. This trailblazing medical breakthrough was vividly described in "The Painful Story Behind Modern Anesthesia" by Dr. Howard Markel. Since then, during surgical operations, anesthetics have been used to help people avoid the excruciating pain that comes with opening up and closing the human body as was the case in the earlier years of medical practice.

We sometimes wish there was a way we can go through life devoid of pain and disappointment but it is not possible. Life offers no anesthesia to prevent pain. You are not a robot or an artificial intelligence-based machine that does not have emotions. Therefore, you will have to learn to marshal your emotions and control your feelings to avoid emotional and psychological bankruptcy. Both strangers and your loved ones will do or say things that will hurt you, no matter how much you care about them.

Everyone would love to avoid pain but it is inevitable. The earlier you accept this truth, the better for you. We are most vulnerable to our family and friends; they are close enough to us to say hurtful words and act in ways that make us experience pain. Sometimes, they do those things without realizing that they are hurting us. Some other times, they deliberately act malignantly for selfish reasons.

You will experience pain in various ways and you will also observe your loved ones getting hurt. This is the sad reality of life. Accept it and find ways to make the most of your time on earth because it will end at some point, whether you like it or not. Admitting that pain is inevitable is one of the ways you can maximize your time on this planet.

Why Pain Is Inevitable

You will find yourself experiencing physical or emotional pain at some point or another during your journey on earth. Below are some reasons pain is inevitable:

You Are Not Immortal

When you watch superhero movies such as Superman, you might wish you had the impeccability of the man of steel whose only weakness is kryptonite. Nonetheless, such wishes only belong to the realm of fantasy. In reality, we are all human beings whose time on earth is numbered. We are like time bombs that will eventually explode when the time is up. We are made of flesh and blood.

Besides, we are wired with emotions. Our feelings are two-edged swords. They are the reasons we can experience beautiful emotions such as love, affection, respect, honor, and value. Sadly, they are also why we can experience negative feelings such as depression, despair, regret, and low self-esteem. It all shows that we are human. Impeccability and perfection do not exist with or among us. We experience pain and also make others suffer. It is our curse and we cannot be cured of it.

You Are Vulnerable To Your Loved Ones

One of the first things you will realize in life is that you are part of a family. You did not choose them. If many of us were given that right, poor people might never have children. We would have chosen to be in the family of celebrities and influential people even if that might not be what is best for us. Variety is the spice of life and the diversity of families and races are meant to show us the beauty in slight differences and variations.

Our family is our first community. They are the first set of people we have around us before we make friends with individuals who share similar values with us. Our friends and families contribute significantly to our happiness and self-esteem. A Harvard study showed that relationships with our loved ones are the greatest source of happiness. Nonetheless, our vulnerability to these people guarantees that we will get hurt at some point by them.

You Are A Logical Being

Come to think of it, the first reason you could get hurt is the fact that you can understand the actions and words of others. If you are a Chinese man and a person says you are stupid in the English language, it is not likely that you will feel insulted, unless someone interprets the meaning of those words to you.

In the same way, if a person pulls a middle finger in your direction, you might not see anything wrong with it if that is your first time noticing that gesture and not knowing its intended meaning. Therefore, our ability to make sense of the things happening around us and the things people do to us is also the same reason we will inevitably experience pain. Whether physically or virtually, you will find insensitive people who will say things and act in ways that will make you understandably emotionally disturbed.

You Have A Memory

Some events hurt us immediately after we process them, while some will give us pain as we try to process them in the future. For example, the loss of a loved one is not an event you will forget quickly. You might find yourself crying years later when you remember them. You want to be with them again but it is no longer possible. All you have of them are memories.

Life would have been easier if we could not remember our past, especially traumatic events. However, we would have to throw away the baby with the bathwater in doing so. Our memories are also full of beautiful events such as our marriage, the birth of our children, and the kind words people said to us. So, we will have to enjoy the good memories and find ways to process the sad events to live a balanced and meaningful life.

Life Is Unpredictable

The precarious nature of life is one of the reasons pain is inevitable. Every trade or weather forecast is an intellectual prediction. Nothing is guaranteed in life. We want to spend our lives in the loving arms of our spouse but sometimes these people hurt us and even elope with our best friends! The only thing that is certain in life is that we will not make it off this earth alive.

Anything is possible in this volatile market called life. Life is like the stock market – it rises and falls at will. This unpredictability is the reason it is never recommended to put all your eggs in one basket. If you make absolute plans and expect that things will never change, you are setting yourself up for a rude shock. Life is full of pleasant surprises and it can also bewilder you negatively.

Chapter Two: Suffering Is Optional

"Forgiveness is a gift you give yourself."

Suzanne Somers

Indeed, some events can be disappointing and traumatic. Nonetheless, the truth is that none of your experiences are peculiar to you. In Lonely, rapper NF said:

"Yeah, does anyone feel like me? Show of hands, I don't need a lot, I just wanna find my peace.

As seen in his words, knowing that you are not alone in your troubles and moments of experience is comforting. In the first chapter, we discussed the fact that pain is inevitable. The focal point of this section is to help you to understand that suffering is optional despite the inevitability of painful experiences.

Pain Is A Teacher

When you experience hurtful situations, it is natural that you will be affected emotionally. Nonetheless, every storm comes with positives if only you can master the art of gratitude and optimism. A change of perspective is all that you need to see the pain in the right light. Once you achieve this, you will not have to suffer simply because you experience a negative occurrence. Here are some ways you can perceive the pain that can help you prevent suffering:

Challenges Reveal Your Strengths

According to the Bible, you have little strength on the day of adversity. Painful events come to show you how strong or weak you are. So, challenges are opportunities to know your strengths and areas of weakness that need improvement. Until you have experienced certain events, your perceived ability to cope is a mere assumption. How do you react to a divorce, loss of a job, loss of a loved one, or betrayal?

Will you lose your cool or move on? Will you collapse mentally or fight to make the best of your life? You can never know the answers to these questions until you experience these events. It is fantastic to have plans for your reactions; however, some things are easier said than done. So, when you find yourself in an unpleasant situation, remember that it is a test of your mental strength.

Turbulence Makes You Stronger

Difficult times generally make you stronger, especially when you react appropriately to them. Even when you fail the test, you learn how difficult it is to deal with certain issues and that will prepare you for the future. In the Bible, Peter denied Jesus because he was afraid he might lose his life.

Jesus had warned him earlier but he overrated himself. Despite his failure, that event showed him his weakness and he became more committed to the cause of his Lord, even after Jesus was gone. So, even when you react badly to a sad occurrence, such as the betrayal of a friend, it will not hurt as much as the first time if you ever have such experiences again.

Adversity Makes You A Source Of Inspiration

Whenever people are experiencing turbulent times, they always look for sources of inspiration that can give them hope. For example, when you experience a divorce, it is natural that you want to find examples of people who have gone through such situations but are living happily. We leverage this approach because it helps us to approach our current circumstances with optimism.

We all need hope and you can be a source of encouragement to others through the things you experience. These people might approach you or discuss their situation with you. However, they can learn a lot by observing you from a distance or reading your story. Your experience can be the benchmark of how to handle difficult times even for generations unborn as yet. Therefore, you should think about the kind of example you set through your decisions.

Pain Makes You A Mentor

In some situations, you will deliberately or inadvertently become a mentor to some people due to a painful experience you had in the past. For example, the father of Valued Investing, Benjamin Gram, lost a lot of money in his early years as an entrepreneur. Such an occurrence would have made some people give up on investments but that was not the case with him. Instead, he leveraged the experience to learn a better approach to investing.

The lessons he drew from the unfortunate event eventually made him the mentor of several successful investors such as Warren Buffet. So, you never can tell who might need to learn from your experience. People find it easier to trust your guidance when you have recovered from the same events that are threatening to ruin their lives. So, don't waste your pain. Instead of suffering, use your setbacks to mentor others to avoid the same pitfalls you fell into.

Troubles Are Blessings In Disguise

Benjamin Graham wrote two books based on his experience as an investor. Never forget that his loss is a critical part of his latter success. He probably might never have become an author and successful investor if he didn't lose his money in the past. So, sometimes, our setbacks are the foundations of our future success.

Your mistakes and how you recovered from them teach you valuable life lessons that many people will want to learn from. Besides, some negative events are what catapult us to the next level. For example, being sacked has made several people into great entrepreneurs. The author of Harry Potter, J.K. Rowling, is a great example of this. She had more time to complete her manuscript after she was sacked from her role as the secretary of a company.

Pain Will Make You Empathetic

One of the beautiful aspects of failure is that it makes you empathetic towards others. If you have made mistakes before, you will be more patient with others when they commit errors. For example, if you had issues with your marriage, you will be less critical of people who experience a divorce. You will not join the bandwagon of critics hurling insults at such people.

So, sometimes, one of the ways life humbles us to be patient and empathetic towards others is through the experience of disappointing situations. Your failure gives you a better advantage that will make you take measured approaches when reacting to the challenging moments of others. When you are experiencing turbulence, you want a hand on your shoulder encouraging you. You will want to do the same for others if you have enjoyed such favors in the past.

Turbulence Can Enhance Your Stability And Loyalty

Some people will never learn to respect their professional and interpersonal relationships unless they have experienced betrayals and disloyalties in the past. You will never understand how difficult it is to recover from a heartbreak unless someone you loved did not reciprocate your affection and commitment.

The moment you experience heartbreak, it is likely that you are more careful to avoid putting others through the same situation. The fallout of such occurrences is that you might become more stable and loyal to your friends and family. So, pain does not have to become suffering if you only have the right perspective. What you need is a paradigm shift if sad situations have made you suffer a lot in the past.

Chapter Three: Dissecting Emotions

"One ought to hold on to one's heart; for if one lets it go, one soon loses control of the head too."

Friedrich Nietzsche

We are beginning to get to the crux of the purpose of this book. If you always act based on how you feel, you will become impulsive, which can lead to disastrous decisions. Suicide is one of the worst options for some people because of their inability to master their emotions. This is the reason Nietzsche said in the quote above that we will lose our heads when we don't hold on to our hearts. This chapter will discuss what emotions are, why we feel the way we do, and how we can dominate our feelings.

Why Am I Feeling This Way?

According to the Oxford dictionary, emotions are strong feelings that are based on the current circumstances, relationships with others, and mood of a person. Currently, scientists do not have a consensual definition of the concept of emotion. Nonetheless, what is certain is that they are based on situations, our thoughts, and our perceptions. They can be positive or negative.

Positive emotions include happiness, affection, elation, pleasure, and excitement. Meanwhile, negative emotions include sadness, anxiety, depression, and fear. Regardless of the type of emotion you have, you cannot trust your feelings. They can be antithetical to logic most times. For example, you could find yourself tempted to laugh when something tragic happened to a person. Such moments make us feel like the Joker character in Batman's movies. On the other hand, you could have the desire to cry when you know that it is not worth it.

Emotions are contagious. When you stay around people who find something wrong with everything, their pessimistic nature can take away your smile and make you gloomy. On the other hand, when you are around cheerful people, you find it easier to be happy, regardless of your challenges.

The Dangers Of Impulsiveness

There is no limit to the damage you can cause yourself and the people around you when you do not have control over your emotions. Below are some ways you can hurt yourself, your loved ones, or colleagues when you do not master your emotions:

Relationship Issues

Acting suddenly, on impulse, without reflecting on its consequences, can endanger the relationship of a person with friends, family members, business associates, and the public at large. Keeping a cordial and effective relationship with people is vital in ensuring the social growth of an individual. However, during conversations, there are high tendencies of getting offended intentionally or unintentionally.

Acting on these impulses ought to be reflected upon before acting or giving replies. Failure to reflect on the consequences of actions can lead to quarrels which will destroy the relationship with friends or loved ones. Therefore, while we interact with individuals, we need to be watchful of how we converse or make jokes. Considering the personal likes and dislikes of people will go a long way to ensure that you do not develop issues in your relationship with them.

Unstable Mental Health

Constant unchecked behaviors that portray change of action due to impulses can lead to unstable mental health. The brain is the main source of mental health. Whenever a person constantly acts on impulse without reflection, people tend to separate themselves from such individuals. This can lead to loneliness.

Loneliness is not recommended because it usually leads to overthinking, which can cause hypertension. Instead of relating physically with people, these individuals will only have such thoughts in their heads because they do not have anyone to talk to. Compilation of many thoughts in one's head, constantly, can make one become unstable and can lead to mental illness.

Marital Instability

The success or failure of any marriage depends on the level of communication between partners. Communication in marriage can sometimes be cordial and at other times, it can be overwhelming. The ability to control one's impulses during marital interactions is vital. In situations where there is a contradicting idea between partners, it can lead to arguments and can cause negative use of words. The inability to control one's feelings in this situation can lead to domestic violence and make partners resent each other. The marriage becomes unstable because of impulsiveness.

Loneliness

Surrounding yourself with friends and loved ones is the solution to loneliness. However, interaction with these individuals should be carefully handled because the slightest provocation by you can make them distance themselves from you. Impulsiveness can reduce a person's companionship with others. The inability to control one's emotions during interactions will make people drift far from an individual which will cause reduced companionship.

Meanwhile, the lack of companionship is one major factor that leads to loneliness. When there is nobody to talk to, when going through some difficult situations, there is a high tendency of becoming lonely. As the saying goes, "a problem shared is a problem halved" but when there is nobody to share the problems with, then the problems will continue to abound.

Failed Customer Relationships

Communication helps to create a good environment for customers and producers to converse and exchange ideas. It is a known fact that the customer relations of an organization play a vital role in its success because the revenue of a company depends on the rate at which the customers buy its products. Therefore, an organization must never take this aspect for granted.

Most customers come with complaints rather than compliments. The ability to control one's emotions whenever a customer comes to complain about a product or service rendered goes a long way to ensuring a good customer relationship. Impulsiveness can endanger the relationship with customers.

In instances where a customer approaches you with complaints that seem aggressive, it is necessary to control your emotions to give a positive reply. Failure to control your emotions can result in the exchange of negative words that can lead to the loss of customers. Customers determine the success or failure of a business, so it is very vital to keep a good relationship with customers.

Imprisonment

In our daily interactions with people and our environment, there is a high tendency that in the course of interactions we offend each other. Whenever we come across confrontations, we ought to be reserved and mindful of the words we speak to people. Words are like missiles; you cannot retract them once you release them.

Wrongly acting on impulses when angered can cause conflict, which in turn can lead to physical assault. Meanwhile, physical assault is an offense that is punishable under the constitution of any nation and can lead to imprisonment. Therefore, impulsiveness, when not well checked, can lead to imprisonment.

Negative Popularity

It is a good thing to be globally popular and famous, but being infamous due to a negative occurrence or behavior does not bode well for an individual. Acting suddenly on impulse, without reflecting on its consequences can make the entire society comment negatively about that person.

In the case of popular figures in society, celebrities ensure that they maintain a cordial and positive relationship with people in society. However, in cases where they react impulsively to confrontations or occurrences, it will immediately tarnish their image and allow negative comments to be spread about them. Therefore, it is essential to control impulses during daily interactions with people and the environment, to avoid negative reactions and loss of popularity.

Chapter Four: You Are Not A Victim!

"It's not an easy journey to get to a place where you forgive people but it is such a powerful place because it frees you."

Tyler Perry

Slavery and imprisonment go beyond being confined to a place or solitude. You are a slave to your emotions when you always do what you feel. It is an approach to life that can land you in hot water. It can ruin your interpersonal and professional relationships as discussed in the last chapter. In this section, we will explore some proven tips that can help you have more control over your feelings.

Mastering Your Emotions

In the words of Oscar Wilde:

"I don't want to be at the mercy of my emotions. I want to use them, to enjoy them, and to dominate them."

If you don't master your emotions, they can make you do crazy things. The ability to stay calm and make logical decisions despite feeling otherwise is described as **Emotional Intelligence** (EQ) by psychologists. Meanwhile, we are no different from animals when we are impulsive. Animals have sex whenever they feel like it. They eat whatever they find even when it does not belong to them.

The good news is that you can improve your EQ. You will find the following tips useful:

Detect The Source Of The Feeling

Just like stress management, one of the best ways to rule your emotions is to understand why you feel the way you do. Why are you angry? Asking this kind of question helps you to take charge of your emotions. Like an expert detective, you will discover the "criminal" vandalizing your mood.

The same approach goes for feelings of emotions. Don't be happy for no reason just to ensure that the good times are sustainable. Whenever a person tells me that they love me for reasons they can't determine, I am scared. Even romantic feelings have a basis that you need to understand to ensure that you commit for the right reasons. It is safer to ask yourself why you think you are in love with a person.

Is it because the person is sexy and has the kind of killer shape you desire? Is it because the person is intelligent and smart? You need to know. If not, then when that aspect of the person fades away due to life-changing circumstances or aging, your commitment will also fade and wane. This is one of the reasons marriages break down today. Marriage statistics in the US today tell the sad story of how our relationships are built on fickle things and emotions in this modern world.

Is It Worth It?

This question applies to both positive and negative emotions. For example, if you are happy because someone is in love with you or you fell in love with that person, you need to ask yourself whether it is worth it before you go deeper. In the same way, do not accept a job offer to prove a point to a person.

If it is not an ideal role for you, you will quit when things get tougher. Also, the fact that a person said or did something nasty to you is not enough reason to act aggressively. If you commit a crime in the process, you will regret it if it leads to your imprisonment.

Consider The Long-Term Impact

The lack of consequential thinking is the reason people act rashly and make decisions that end in regret. Your emotions should not make you take decisions that can mar your life forever. Before you act aggressively, consider the long-term impact of your action.

In the same way, before you give out your possessions or will away your property, consider what might happen in the long run. Will you be happy with yourself in the next ten years after making this decision? This kind of question can restore your sanity when you are about to act rashly.

Consider The Long-Term Sustainability

People make rash decisions when they are extremely happy or extremely sad. Sometimes, they make promises and commitments they will not be able to sustain. If a person falls in love with you during their low moments or moments when they are extremely happy, it can be dangerous. Reality will soon set in and they might realize that you were never the best option for them, once they are sober.

So, whenever you are happy or sad, be careful before you commit because you might only be listening to your heart and not your head. If you cannot see yourself doing something in the next ten years, then don't start it. If you start a business because the idea sounds brilliant and makes you happy, you might quit anytime soon if you do not consider the long-term sustainability of the vision.

Do Something Else

Whenever you are sad or anxious, consider doing something else for a short while. As a student in college, I would strive hard to achieve academic success. However, whenever I observed that I was under pressure or tense, I would play games for a short time.

Research has proven that anxiety impairs performance by reducing the efficiency of your memory. When you are anxious, you can forget the spelling of a word you have used often; it can be that bad. So, when you are depressed or experiencing negative emotions, engage in a hobby to change your mood.

Also, if you find out that your current career path does not make you happy, you do not have to continue for the sake of it. Try something else. You might not even earn as much as in your current role but it might be the key to your happiness.

Open Up To Others

Speaking to other people is a form of therapy, according to psychologists. Have you ever met strangers talking to you about sensitive things in their lives? I have had such experiences multiple times. I understand what they are trying to do even though I find it weird. They are simply looking for an outlet to pour out their heart.

No matter how disappointing a situation is, you will feel better when you tell other people, even when they do not have the solution to your problem. Of course, you should be selective about your choice of people when considering self-disclosure. Some people are wolves in sheep's clothing; they pretend to be your friend but are only seeking opportunities to bring you down. If a person has not displayed integrity with less sensitive issues in the past, it is not recommended to trust such people with your secret pain.

Seek Professional Help

If you have tried all you could and nothing is changing, it is recommended that you seek the help of a counselor. Such people are trained to help you dissect your emotions and offer you therapies that can remedy the situation. If your feelings have been getting you into trouble and all your efforts to make things better have been futile so far, it is time to talk to an expert. You might be sessions away from controlling your emotions and living a happy life.

Chapter Five: Preventing Pain And Suffering

"Forgive your enemy but never forget their names."

John F. Kennedy

As the old saying postulates, "Prevention is better than cure." If you do not associate yourself with people or situations that will create pain or suffering, then you will have no reason to feel these emotions. Happiness is a priceless gift that every individual strives for daily. Preventing pain and suffering is the only way to obtain happiness. In this chapter, we will take a broad view of the ways to avoid getting hurt and how prevention supersedes cure.

Prevention Supersedes Treatment

It is easier to stop something bad from happening in the first place than to fix the damage after it has happened; as the saying goes, "a stitch in time saves nine." It is terrible to be impulsive. Nonetheless, it is better to have no reasons to exercise self-control. In other words, no one would even know that you lack self-control to a certain degree if you did not place yourself in circumstances that require you to keep your cool.

Note that the things that can hurt you the most, come from the actions of others towards you. Therefore, if you can be more deliberate about your relationships and the kinds of people you have around you, you can prevent over 90 percent of your frustrations.

How To Avoid Getting Hurt

Grief is unpredictable, and it affects everybody in different ways. To avoid venturing into situations or things that will create pain is far better than locating ways to patch it up after the occurrence of pain. To avoid getting hurt, you need to do the following:

Surround Yourself With Positive, Happy People

Always ensure you gather around cheerful people. This set of people will share an atmosphere of happiness. Companions like your family, friends, and many others who have a positive mindset can help to prevent hurt or pain. Keeping them closer to you will help ensure that you have a positive mindset.

Set Personal Boundaries

Establishing clear boundaries helps to prevent similar problems in the future. Strict adherence to rules that will help to guide your relationship with people will enable you to be safe from pain or hurt. It is up to you to assert yourself and let others know what you expect from a friendship or relationship. Define your relationship with people and ensure you communicate your boundaries clearly to them.

Do What You Enjoy

One of the reasons people get frustrated in life is that they do things that do not align with their strengths. You will only end up frustrated when you have a career path or choose hobbies that do not reflect your abilities. You will struggle to excel in them and your failure will lead to frustration.

It is very necessary to always remember the activities you enjoy performing and recognize any positive things happening in your life. Reconnection with close friends or family members, or even a pet will go a long way to help in creating happiness. Keeping your mindset fixed on appreciating good things will energize the mind and safeguard the mind from getting negative thoughts.

Think Positively

There is a need to always have positive thoughts or mindsets when dealing with unpleasant situations. When you are used to thinking negatively, it can be hard to make a change to positive thinking. You can change the way you think by easily replacing negative thoughts with more positive and realistic ones. Positive thinking will ensure that your mindset is positioned in a way that will hinder negative thoughts from coming to your mind.

The help of a mindful or mental health expert can help you practice guided principles to aid in achieving happiness. Therapy is a good way to solve the problem of pain or hurt. A therapist will guide and encourage you in strategies you should follow to ensure daily freedom from pain and suffering.

Develop A Positive Sense Of Humor

Humor helps to keep the mind and emotions fixed. It reduces emotional pain as it shifts how one feels, thinks, and creates bonds. Humor increases physical pain tolerance through distraction. Learn to see the funny side of life to retain a positive mindset that will help you to ward off the wrong actions of other people towards you. It is a kind of buffer that keeps you safe from negative emotions.

Meditation

Learning to accept your emotions can make emotional regulation easier. Meditation helps to increase acceptance skills. It also helps to increase your awareness of all feelings and experiences. Whenever you are meditating, you are teaching yourself to sit with your feelings and recognize them without criticizing or trying to modify or suppress them.

The objective of meditation is to help you relax better and to enable you to get enough sleep. This activity puts you in the right state of mind, making it difficult for you to react in a way that might lead to regrets in the future. Many celebrities understand the benefits of this practice and they are proudly enjoying it.

Chapter Six: Recovering From Past Hurts

"When a deep injury is done to us, we never recover until we forgive."
Alan Paton

One of the reasons many people struggle to deal with negative thoughts is that they have not healed from past hurts. They bottle up their pain and readily unleash terror on others whenever the opportunity presents itself. When you see the harsh words and bullying behavior of some people on social media platforms, it is obvious that these are individuals who have rarely experienced love and affection in their lives. Here are some tips that will help you heal from past hurts:

Be Courageous

In *The Body Keeps The Score,* author Bessel van der Kolk, M.D explained that one of the best ways to deal with traumatic events is to be courageous enough to process your thoughts. Whether you are deliberate about it or not, thoughts will run through your mind as long as you are alive. Therefore, you must take control of them to avoid stirring up destructive emotions.

When you do not get hold of your thoughts, your mind can wander into anger, nudity, fear, anxiety, and sadness. The default mode of most people when they have experienced a traumatic event is avoidance. According to the Kubler-Ross stages of grief, the first stage is denial. They try as much as possible to think about other things because they are scared of the aftermath of their openness to process the event. Nonetheless, you need this bravery because it has helped many people to recover from terrible pasts.

It begins by thinking about the event and all that transpired. You will also consider if there were certain mistakes you made that led to the issue. Then proceed into what you should make of the event. If it is a divorce, convince yourself that you can still make the most of your life despite what happened and make concrete plans to enjoy the rest of your life.

Leverage A Positive Mantra

Words are powerful. They are potent enough to either make you feel good or make you feel terrible. According to clinical psychologist, Carla Manly, Ph.D., the things you say during a setback determine how quickly you will recover from it. Saying things like "This is so terrible! What did I do to deserve this?" is not recommended. As long as you keep hammering on the negativity of your experiences, you will struggle to recover from traumatic events.

Instead, switch to something positive. Say something like, "I am not sure what is going on or why this has happened but I am sure that it will chart the course of a new life for me." You will never realize the potency of a statement like this until you start saying it. Even if you don't believe it at first, it will help you to change your perspective and this will eventually affect your emotions.

Stay Away

If you have things that remind you of a person or experience that hurts you, it will be challenging to heal from the pain. According to clinical psychologist, Ramani Durvasula, Ph.D., a physical or psychological distance between you and a person or situation that makes you feel bad is the right decision. It helps you to avoid thinking about the person or event until you dare to process the experience and recover from it.

Even after recovering from a traumatic event, it is best to create a gap between yourself and the person that hurt you to avoid a repetition of the experience unless the person attempts to reconcile with you. Mind you, reconciliation does not always mean you should continue the relationship.

For example, reconciling with an abusive partner should end with wishing the person well and being willing to help the person if you have the opportunity and capacity. Submitting yourself to the person again in the name of reconciliation is tantamount to walking into a trap.

Practice Gratitude

No matter what has happened to you, the truth is that it could have been worse. Naturally, you are sad when you experience a setback or face adversity. Nonetheless, crying and wailing will not change the situation. What we need is not more tears but seeking ways to move on. Practicing gratitude is one of the best ways to do this.

Did you lose your job? It is terrible indeed but it could have been worse. You could have lost your life. Besides, losing one's job is not as traumatic as losing one's family or friends. It might sound extreme but it is your best bet to change your perspective about a sad situation threatening to ruin your peace of mind.

It is recommended that you develop a culture of gratitude during your regular days so that it can become your way of life. If you make gratitude a practice on your normal days, you will find it easier to make it your default mode during your turbulent periods. So, it is better to imbibe this culture long before a disastrous event occurs.

Mindfulness

Mindfulness is a practice that involves focusing on one thing at a time. One of the reasons we are overwhelmed by negative emotions is that we allow our minds to wander to several things at the same time. Human beings are not designed for multitasking. Studies have shown that multitasking reduces our efficiency.

It is easy to get anxious or paralyzed by fear when you are thinking about all the things you need to do at the same time. The funny thing about life is that many of the things that make us afraid end up not happening the way we envisaged them. It is always better to focus on the current reality rather than thinking about the bad things that have happened. You cannot change the past but you can make the best of the present to have a glorious future.

Forgive Yourself And Others

During a setback, you will either blame yourself or other people that hurt you. Regardless of who you think is responsible for your failure, what matters is that you choose to take responsibility for your life. It is okay that you are critical of yourself when you are at fault but it is not recommended to continue berating yourself for long. You should think about how you can move on as soon as possible.

Accept the fact that you are fallible as a human being and extend this grace to others. Choose to forgive the people that contributed to your setback and make concrete plans for a turnaround. As long as you are alive, you will always have multiple opportunities to rise again no matter how many times you fall. As long as you make up your mind to recover, life will allow you to change your life.

Embrace A New Beginning

You have to accept that some things will never be the same after you experience a setback. For example, after losing your job, you will have to admit that certain privileges you have with some people are all gone. Failing to embrace those changes a setback brings to your life will only lead to frustration. Your friends and family might not even rate you as they did in the past. Embrace the fallouts and climb up slowly, enjoying the process.

Chapter Seven: Maximizing Happiness

"Anger begets more anger, and forgiveness and love lead to more forgiveness and love."

Mahavira

You are responsible for your happiness. Waiting for others to make us happy is one of the reasons we experience frustrations and disappointments in marriages, friendships, and our relationships with others. When you make up your mind to move on from a setback, you will experience a certain level of happiness. It will increase when you practice the following:

Acquire New Skills

It is good that you have made up your mind to move on after losing your job. Yet, it is more important that you develop yourself. Studies have shown that self-development improves our mood. It makes you feel that you are getting better and that makes you happier. If you were sacked because you were not able to cope with the job demands, improve yourself and come back stronger.

Acquiring new skills is not fun but it is always worth it. It will boost your self-esteem and will improve your mood when people praise you for your skillfulness. Note that acquiring skills goes beyond learning a musical instrument or training to learn copywriting and graphic design or coding. It can also be in the form of soft skills such as communication skills, listening, management, organization, and conflict resolution.

Beyond your ability to carry out your job effectively in your workplace, you should have other things you contribute. This is one of the factors that makes you indispensable to any organization. So, if you want to be happier, consider the acquisition of new skills that will add value to you as a person.

Increase Existing Skills

Sharpening your current skills is as good as acquiring new ones. Whatever is worth doing in the first place is worth doing excellently. Many people took advantage of the COVID-19 lockdown to acquire new skills and improve existing ones. You might be wondering how that was possible when people were not allowed to go out. The reality is that the Internet has opened us up to endless opportunities to learn and sharpen our skills.

There is virtually nothing you want to learn today that is not available on the

Internet. From musical instruments to online businesses, the Internet is replete with valuable resources that can help you develop your skills. Regardless of your best learning method, you will find verbal, textual, graphical, and visual materials that can help you to improve your skills. So, you have no excuse.

If you prefer to learn physically, you can find a place where you can learn your desired skills or even hire a private tutor. There are several options you can consider. It is even better to learn from a person you can see because that will allow you to ask questions directly. Your teacher will also use his or her experience to guide you. This approach ensures that you avoid unnecessary time wasted due to trial and error.

Me-Time!

No one is meant to exist in solitude. Even animals enjoy each other's company. Life is beautiful when shared with others. Nonetheless, you should have times when you are alone. This period of your day should be set aside for learning, recreation, and reflection. Some of the activities you can include in your me-time include gratitude, journaling, meditation, yoga, workout, and reading. You can also spend this time in your garden or any natural environment.

This practice helps you to take your mind off the troubles of life and to enjoy a peaceful moment by yourself. It can be a period in the day when you plan for the next day. You can also use that time to set short-term and long-term goals. Note that studies have shown that goal setting is a practice that enhances our focus and self-esteem. It gives you a sense of purpose and makes you happier even when you are yet to achieve your dream. Knowing that there is something you are looking forward to achieving is enough motivation to keep you going.

Find A New Hobby

Sometimes we stumble on hobbies and sometimes, we discover them. Your hobby is an activity you enjoy. Of course, you cannot spend most of your day on this activity because it is not likely to offer you monetary value in return. Due to the reality of striving to pay our bills, take care of ourselves, and take responsibility for our loved ones, it is not feasible to spend significant time on our hobbies.

For example, I enjoy playing football but it would be unreasonable of me to spend most parts of my day on football when I am not Lionel Messi. It is possible that you make a career of your hobby and it is always beautiful when that is the case. However, it is not like that for most people. We usually choose careers that can pay our bills because we would not be happy with ourselves if we failed in this aspect. Nonetheless, regardless of your career choice, it is refreshing to create time for your hobbies once in a while.

Make New Friends

You will never realize what you are missing until you change your current circle of friends. Loyalty to friends is a commendable virtue. Nonetheless, there is no point in committing to people that cannot contribute much to your life. Of course, you should not look down on people because they are not financially stable. Friendship is not all about how much the person can give to you. Yet, even if your friends cannot give you money, they should be able to encourage you and give you good counsel.

If all you do with your current circle of friends is drink, party, and gossip, it is high time you consider new friends that can aid your development and help you to maintain your core values. Some people's friends are the reason they have never had stable relationships. Of course, your friends should advise you to leave an abusive relationship. However, you have to be careful to ensure that they do not use the wrong indicators to ruin your relationships.

Don't Let Bad Feelings Linger

No matter how much you choose to be happy, bad days are inevitable. There will always be forgettable events in your life regardless of your commitment to living a happy and meaningful life. Disappointments are part and parcel of life. So, it is always good to prepare your mind for your reactions to those days. Remember that you have a choice. You can choose to be frustrated or choose to look forward to better days.

Optimism and pessimism are choices. You have the right to make choices but not the right to decide the consequences of your actions. Optimism will make you happier, according to studies but pessimism will only make you gloomier. Life will not always give you what you want but you can choose to always make lemonades out of lemons. It is okay to be sad, sometimes, but it is not good to let bad thoughts and feelings linger.

Chapter Eight: Don't Be The Aggressor!

"There is no revenge so complete like forgiveness"

Josh Billings

We have spent most parts of this book discussing how you can control your emotions and prevent people from hurting and manipulating you. Therefore, it is perfect that we conclude this journey by talking about you not inflicting pain on others. It is hypocritical to hate getting hurt when you have a culture of offending others yourself! Relationships only last when both sides agree to love one another and forgive one another when they are hurting.

Remember How It Felt

In *My Best Friend*, a tribute to the legendary Paul Walker, rapper Andy Mineo waxed lyrical about how some people want others to bleed simply because they were hurt. What some people do with their pain is shocking. Instead of allowing themselves to heal from their hurt, they rather inflict the same pain on others who were not the ones that offended them.

For example, some women make up their minds to make several men contract HIV/AIDS simply because they got the virus from a man! Despite the horror of this claim, this is one of the terrifying realities of this world. Many people inflict pain on innocent people as a way to get revenge. It is sad indeed but this is the approach of some people to life.

Some people deliberately allow others to fall in love with them only to break their hearts as a way to show that they have come of age in the romantic industry. Such actions are despicable. It is better to remember how painful the experience was and make up your mind to ensure that no one else goes through the same ordeal. However, many people do not have this approach. It gives them some sort of satisfaction to see others suffer like them.

I once saw the post of a young lady on social media. She was smiling mischievously as she recanted her experience of dating a guy who never reciprocated her love. Guess what she made up her mind to do? She planned to make sure the next person she dated suffered heartbreak! Terrifying, isn't it? If you have been hurt in any way, remember how it felt. Others do not have to bleed simply because they were hurt by someone.

You Have A Choice

"I had no choice but to..." Many people make this statement when describing certain actions they took. It is common but not true. Whatever decision you took was the choice you made, no matter the situation. When people hurt you, you have a choice. You can either choose to heal from the pain and live a better life or bottle up the emotion to hurt others.

When I see the comments of some people on social media, I wonder what they have been through that makes them so insensitive and harsh towards others. I could not believe my eyes when some people were mocking Cristiano Ronaldo after he lost his son! Even if these people don't believe he is a good player, at least, they should remember that we are all humans, and losing a child is painful and can be traumatic.

Choose to heal from your pain. Others do not have to bleed the same way you bled. Let your hurtful experiences help you to understand what others go through. We do not have to become the aggressor as a way of fighting back. As seen in the quote by Josh Billings at the beginning of this chapter, forgiveness is always the best revenge. Studies have shown that this approach has several psychological benefits.

Making The World A Better Place

There are people whose impact has affected the world and changed many lives. Their achievements are laudable and should be celebrated. Nonetheless, making the world a better place begins from where you are. It begins by adding value to the lives of your friends and family. It is wonderful to know how to control your emotions and thoughts but it is more important to know how to put a smile on the face of others. The following tips will help you to achieve this:

Never Stop Forgiving

Perfection should never be the goal because it is a target we will never be able to meet. Therefore, it will be unreasonable to expect that the people around us will always do the right things. They will hurt us sometimes, whether it is intentional or not.

Some of these events can be painful but we will never be able to build a community full of peace when we hold grudges against one another. Life is beautiful when we pay the price of love. Forbearing one another is a critical aspect of love. We have to make up our minds to keep forgiving and loving one another as much as possible.

Be Empathetic

Some people will never learn to be empathetic until they have gone through traumatic events themselves. Nonetheless, that is not the best approach. When the people around us are experiencing challenging periods in their lives, it is not recommended to mock them. Even when we think that their problems are avoidable, we should still make it a point to be empathetic. Endeavor to speak to them, to encourage them. It is your widow's mite.

Be Willing To Make Sacrifices

Some people have the habit of claiming that they do not owe anyone anything. Indeed, it is true that no one should feel entitled to our love and support. Nonetheless, we cannot live together in harmony and enjoy the bliss that comes from interpersonal relationships unless we are willing to make sacrifices for one another.

Sacrifices can come in the form of spending time with sick people, giving money to support the needy, and sharing our properties with others. It can also be in the form of sharing our intellectual property with others. In whatever form, life is more meaningful and beautiful when we let others enjoy certain privileges we have.

Keep Your Promises

If you have ever experienced the heartbreak that comes from failed promises, you will never disappoint people. Of course, certain unforeseen circumstances make it impossible to fulfill certain promises. However, if we are more careful and intentional, we will not make promises we cannot keep.

Think twice before telling a woman or man that you will stay with them forever and never leave. It is never easy to heal from heartbreak. So, do your best to ensure that you are not the reason other people experience such ordeals.

Love Genuinely

Loving people goes beyond words. When your actions do not match your words, you are only being hypocritical. We can make the world a better place when we love sincerely. It begins with our relationships with our loved ones before it eventually extends to our neighbors and colleagues.

Becoming a hero and heroine begins with simple actions such as empathy and commitment that are not based on ulterior motives and personal gain. We can change the world one day at a time by loving others genuinely. Don't wait for anyone. Let the change begin with you.

Conclusion

Just as I promised when we began this journey, I am certain that it has been a worthwhile experience for you. I am sure that you are raring to go as you abandon your old suffering and sulking self. It is a new beginning for you as you approach life with a new, empowering perspective that will infuse optimism and positivity into the rest of your life.

Never forget that pain is inevitable but suffering is avoidable. You will have to make deliberate decisions every day to make the most of your life. Happiness is a choice and it is recommended that you make it your default mode. Life is too short to be lived in regret and sadness. You cannot always control your experiences but you can determine your reaction to every event in your life.

It will be my utmost joy to find out that you have made up your mind to leverage the tips, lessons, and recommendations in this book to enhance your emotional intelligence and have more control over your mood. If you make this choice, you are preparing yourself to enjoy the rest of your life. Let the new era begin! Today is still a great day to be alive!

References

Harrah, S. (2015). *Medical Milestones: Discovery of Anesthesia & Timeline.* UMHS. Retrieved August 20, 2022, from https://www.umhs-sk.org/blog/medical-milestones-discovery-anesthesia-timeline

Johns Hopkins Medicine (2020). *Forgiveness: Your Health Depends on It.* Johns Hopkins Medicine. Retrieved September 22, 2021, from https://www.hopkinsmedicine.org/health/wellness-and-prevention/forgiveness-your-health-depends-on-it

Mejia, Z. (2017, October 31). *Harvard's longest study of adult life reveals how you can be happier and more successful.* CNBC. https://www.cnbc.com/2017/10/31/this-harvard-study-reveals-how-you-can-be-happier-and-more-successful.html

Greater Good (2004). *The New Science of Forgiveness.* Greater Good. https://greatergood.berkeley.edu/article/item/the_new_science_of_forgiveness

Thank you for reading this book!

If you found this book helpful, I would be grateful if you would **post an honest review on Amazon** so this book can reach other supportive readers like you!

All you need to do is digitally flip to the back and leave your review. Or visit amazon.com/author/senseipauldavid click the correct book cover and click on the blue link next to the yellow stars that say, "customer reviews."

As always...
It's a great day to be alive!

Get/Share Our FREE All-Ages Mental Health Book Now!

FREE Self-Development Book for Every Family

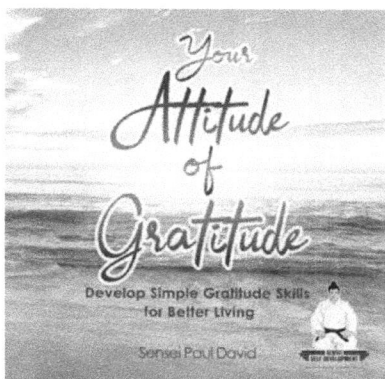

senseiselfdevelopment.senseipublishing.com

Click Below or Search Amazon for Another Book In This Series Or Visit:

www.amazon.com/author/senseipauldavid

SENSEI
SELF DEVELOPMENT
— BOOKS SERIES —

senseiselfdevelopment.senseipublishing.com

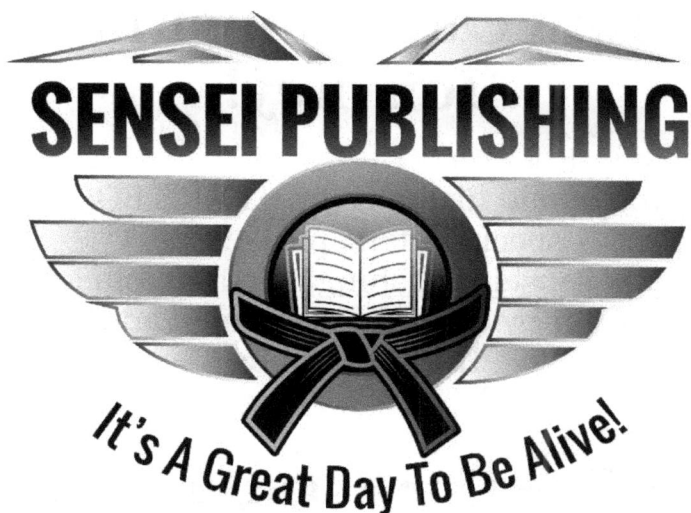

SENSEI PUBLISHING

It's A Great Day To Be Alive!

www.senseipublishing.com

@senseipublishing
#senseipublishing

Check out our **recommendations** for other books for adults & kids plus other great resources by visiting
www.senseipublishing.com/resources/

Join Our Publishing Journey!

If you would like to receive FREE BOOKS, special offers, please visit www.senseipublishing.com and join our newsletter by entering your email address in the pop-up box

Follow Our Engaging Blog NOW! senseipauldavid.ca

Get Our FREE Books Today!

Click & Share the Link Below

FREE Self-Development Book
senseiselfdevelopment.senseipublishing.com

FREE BONUS!!!
Experience Over 25 FREE Engaging
Guided Meditations!

Prized Skills & Practices for Adults & Kids.
Help Restore Deep-Sleep, Lower Stress,
Improve Posture, Navigate Uncertainty &
More.

Download the Free Insight Timer App and click
the link below:
http://insig.ht/sensei_paul

About Sensei Publishing

Sensei Publishing commits itself to helping people of all ages transform into better versions of themselves by providing high-quality and research-based self-development books with an emphasis on mental health and guided meditations. Sensei Publishing offers well-written e-books, audiobooks, paperbacks and online courses that simplify complicated but practical topics in line with its mission to inspire people towards positive transformation.

It's a great day to be alive!

About the Author

I create simple & transformative eBooks & Guided Meditations for Adults & Children proven to help navigate uncertainty, solve niche problems & bring families closer together.

I'm a former finance project manager, private pilot, jiu-jitsu instructor, musician & former University of Toronto Fitness Trainer. I prefer a science-based approach to focus on these & other areas in my life to stay humble & hungry to evolve. I hope you enjoy my work and I'd love to hear your feedback.

- It's a great day to be alive!
Sensei Paul David

Scan & Follow/Like/Subscribe: Facebook, Instagram,
YouTube: @senseipublishing

Scan using your phone/iPad camera for Social Media
Visit us at www.senseipublishing.com and sign up for
our newsletter to learn more about our exciting books
and to experience our FREE Guided Meditations for
Kids & Adults.